SCHIRMER'S LIBRARY
OF MUSICAL CLASSICS

Vol. 1031

HERMANN BERENS

Op. 89

Training of the Left Hand

Forty-Six Exercises and
Twenty-Five Studies
for Left Hand Alone

English Translations by
DR. THEODORE BAKER

✦

ISBN 978-0-7935-5224-5

G. SCHIRMER, Inc.

DISTRIBUTED BY
HAL•LEONARD®
CORPORATION
7777 W. BLUEMOUND RD. P.O. BOX 13819 MILWAUKEE, WI 53213

Printed in the U.S.A. by G. Schirmer, Inc.

Training of the Left Hand

Forty-six Exercises and Twenty-five Studies
For Left Hand Alone
Book I: Forty-six Exercises

It is the aim of these exercises to impart velocity, strength and evenness of touch to the fingers. Any one having the patience to take up six or eight numbers daily and practise them from ten to fifteen minutes, will soon be convinced of their usefulness. Begin in a moderate tempo, increasing it at each repetition.

English translations by
Dr. Th. Baker

H. Berens. Op. 89, Book 1

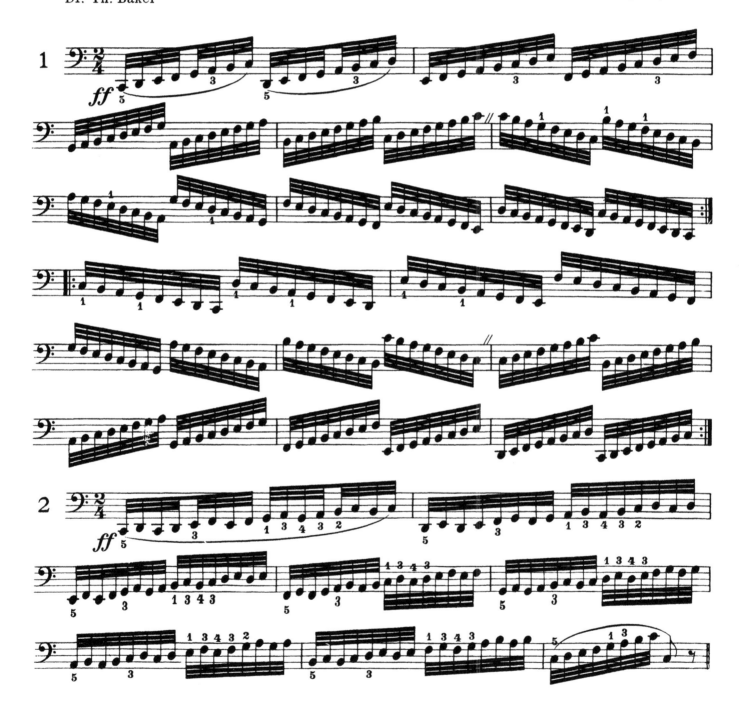

Printed in the U.S.A. by G. Schirmer, Inc.

4

Where two fingerings are given, they should be practised alternately.

17

18

19

8

20

21

22

23

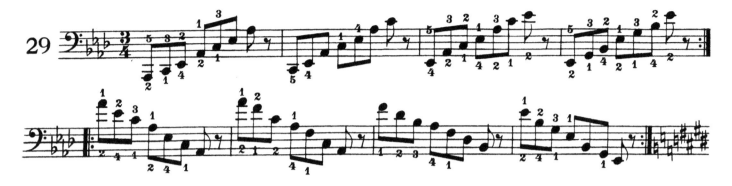

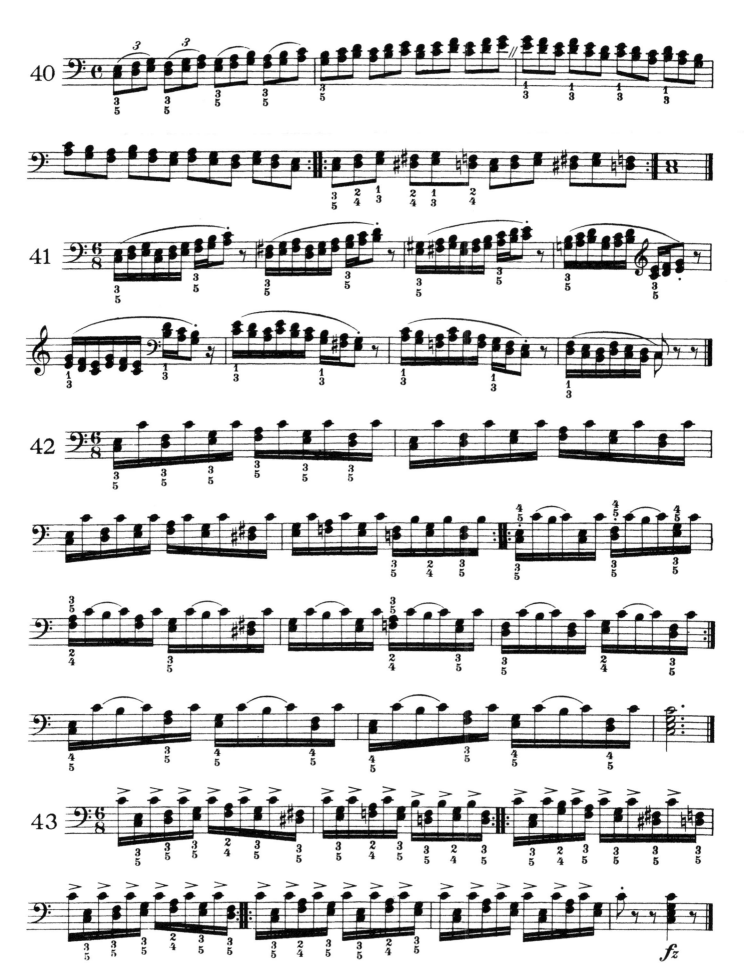

44

45

46

Book II: Twenty-five Studies

H. Berens. Op. 89, Book II

Allegro
sempre legato

3

poco ritard.

Moderato cantabile

22

Allegro moderato

14

28

Allegro vivace

21

Allegro

22

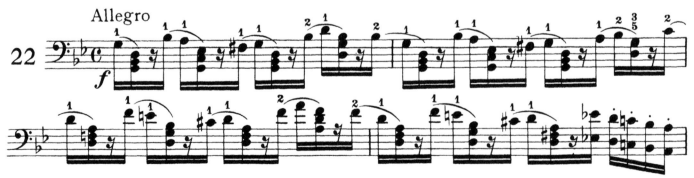

Andante espressivo

23